Forgotten Heroes of the American Revolution

JOHN STARK

Live Free or Die

FORGOTTEN HEROES
OF THE AMERICAN REVOLUTION

Nathanael Greene: The General Who Saved the Revolution

Henry Knox: Washington's Artilleryman

Francis Marion: Swamp Fox of South Carolina

Daniel Morgan: Fighting Frontiersman

John Stark: Live Free or Die

Forgotten Heroes of the American Revolution

JOHN STARK

Live Free or Die

Karl Crannell

OTTN PUBLISHING
STOCKTON, NJ

DEDICATION: To Mrs. Bentley and Mrs. Fordyce, my third and sixth grade teachers, who saw potential where others saw misbehavior; and my wife, Amy, who still does.

Frontispiece: American soldiers commanded by John Stark captured this sword, drum, and cartridge box at the Battle of Bennington.

OTTN Publishing
16 Risler Street
Stockton, NJ 08859
www.ottnpublishing.com

3 5 7 9 8 6 4 2

Library of Congress Cataloging-in-Publication Data

Crannell, Karl, 1953-
  John Stark : live free or die! / Karl Crannell.
      p. cm. — (Forgotten heroes of the American Revolution)
  Summary: "A biography of the Revolutionary War leader from New Hampshire who played a decisive role in several clashes, including Bunker Hill and the Battle of Bennington"—Provided by publisher.
  Includes bibliographical references and index.
  ISBN-13: 978-1-59556-016-2 (hc)
  ISBN-10: 1-59556-016-5 (hc)
  ISBN-13: 978-1-59556-021-6 (pb)
  ISBN-10: 1-59556-021-1 (pb)
  1. Stark, John, 1728-1822—Juvenile literature. 2. Generals—United States—Biography—Juvenile literature. 3. United States—History—Revolution, 1775-1783—Biography—Juvenile literature. 4. United States—History—Revolution, 1775-1783—Campaigns—Juvenile literature. 5. United States. Continental Army—Biography—Juvenile literature. I. Title.
  E207.S79C73 2006
  973.3'3092—dc22
  [B]
                                        2006021059

Publisher's Note: All quotations in this book come from original sources, and contain the spelling and grammatical inconsistencies of the original text.

TABLE OF CONTENTS

Why John Stark Should Be Remembered

"It is with singular Pleasure I congratulate you and your brave militia on the Honour which you have acquir'd at the important Battle of Bennington. I feel it the More gratefully as it has eminently contributed to rescue this devoted State from the dangers with which it was surrounded."

> —New York Continental Congress delegate James Duane,
> letter to John Stark, December 16, 1777

"To John Stark . . . belongs the credit of having been the only man, during the war of independence, who, at a head of a body of militia, stormed and carried entrenchments defended by veteran troops. . . . Much of the glory of this achievement belongs exclusively to Stark, whose influence over his raw levies was miraculous, and whose skill availed itself of every possible contingency in his favor. In short, the hero of Bennington was one of the ablest military men of the Revolution."

> —Charles J. Peterson, in *The Military Heroes of the Revolution
> with a Narrative of the War of Independence* (1848)

"There is a peculiar kind of heroism about the character of John Stark as it is handed down to the historian. . . . It is the heroism of a strongly marked individuality—of a gentle nature covered over by a rough exterior. There is a kind of latter day-chivalry enveloping the accounts we have of him, which, in the times of tournament and spear, would have passed current as the true gold of knighthood."

> —Willard Glazier, in *Heroes of Three Wars: Comprising a Series of Bio-
> graphical Sketches of the Most Distinguished Soldiers of the War of the
> Revolution, the War with Mexico, and the War for the Union, Who Have
> Contributed by Their Valor to Establish and Perpetuate
> the Republic of the United States* (1880)

"In this battle [Trenton] Stark was a conspicuous figure. It is said that the New Hampshire troops under him displayed great gallantry."

> —Senator Jacob H. Gallinger, address to the United States Senate
> on the acceptance of the statue of John Stark into the
> National Statuary Hall Collection, 1894

"At Bennington . . . Stark won one of the most spectacular and decisive successes of the Revolution. . . . [He] had an uncanny way of being at the critical and unexpected place to ruin British plans, first at Bunker Hill, then at Bennington, and finally at Saratoga."

—Mark Mayo Boatner, in *Encyclopedia of the American Revolution* (1994)

"John Stark was a man of violent courage. It was said of him that, like a hunting dog, the hackles of hair on the back of his neck would stand out straight when he contemplated a fight; and like so many of the other veteran officers, fighting had been his avocation and preoccupation most of his adult years. . . . He was a born leader of men . . . always outspoken, with intuitive judgment gained from combat experience. Through the next few years of the Revolution, his services were to be of extreme and critical value."

—Charles H. Bradford, in *Battle Road and Charlestown Heights: Lost and Won*, edited by Carl W. Mores (2003)

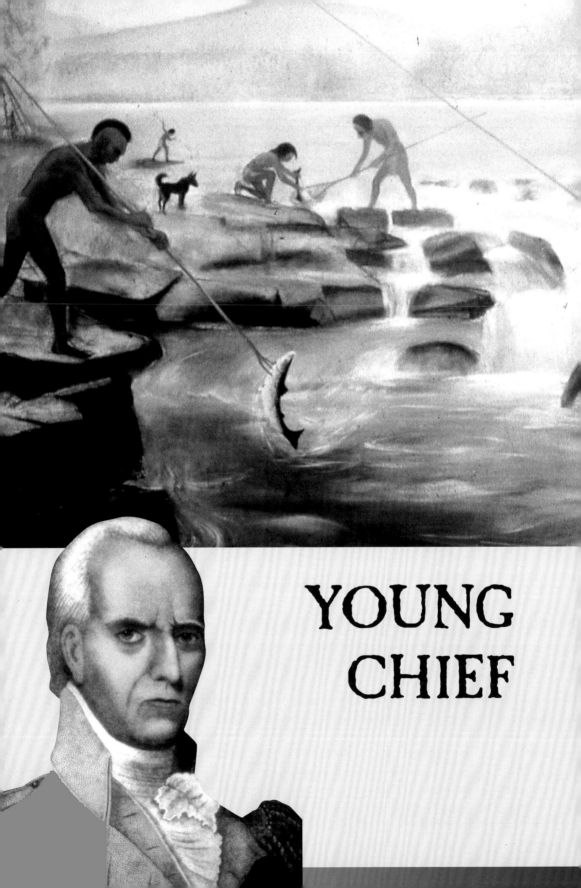

YOUNG
CHIEF

This 19th-century watercolor painting shows Abenaki men fishing in the Merrimack River. The Abenaki tribe lived in the area of modern-day New Hampshire and Vermont, and they often joined the French to fight English settlers in North America. As a young man, John Stark (opposite) was captured by Abenakis while on a hunting trip.

I n March 1752, when John Stark was 24 years old, he went on a hunting and trapping trip with his older brother, William, and two friends, David Stinson and Amos East-man. The trip would be long and would take them to the center of the New Hampshire *province* (near present-day Rumney, New Hampshire). They traveled on foot, following rivers and streams, but they also had a canoe. When they reached their destination, they set up camp. They built shelters of hemlock branches and tree bark in which they would sleep and store their supplies of food and ammunition. The trip was a great success. They collected many valuable furs from the animals they trapped.

On April 27, they saw signs that another hunting party was in the area, and they were certain the other hunters were Indians. Wanting to avoid trouble, the Stark brothers, Stinson, and Eastman decided that it would be best for them to leave. The next day, they began packing up and loading their canoe for the journey home. John Stark, being the youngest member of the group, was sent to collect all the traps that had been laid out. By sunset on April 28, Stark had nearly completed his task. As he bent down to pick up a trap, he heard a sound like the hissing of a snake, then a rustling in the bushes. He looked up. Ten muskets, cocked and ready to fire, were pointed right at him. It was too late to run or reach for his musket. He was surrounded by Indians.

PRISONER OF THE ABENAKIS

John Stark was now a prisoner of the Abenaki tribe. The leader of the group shouted questions at Stark in broken English. He asked the young man about his friends and demanded to know where their camp was. Stark knew that he could be killed at any moment, but he remained calm and defiant. He pointed in the opposite direction.

Back in camp, the other hunters discussed what they should do. Their companion had been gone too long, and they were worried that something had happened to him. They fired their muskets into the air, hoping to hear Stark fire his musket in response. At that moment, he was two miles from camp, leading his Abenaki captors farther and farther away. Hearing the shots, the Indians knew instantly what to do. They headed for the river and climbed into their canoes. It was nighttime now, and in the darkness, they were able to float quietly down the river and past the white hunters' camp without being discovered. Landing a little below the camp, the Abenakis took up positions along the riverbank and waited in ambush for the hunters.

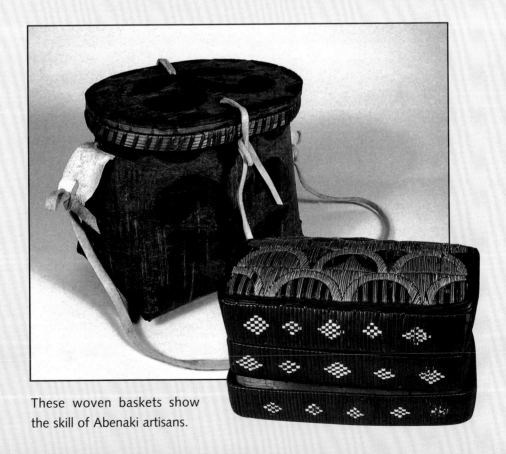

These woven baskets show the skill of Abenaki artisans.

By the morning of April 29, 1752, John Stark's com-
panions were sure he had been captured or killed by the
Indians they knew were nearby. They decided to search for
him downriver. William Stark and Stinson would take the
canoe, while Eastman would go by land, sticking close to
the riverbank. Eastman had walked only a short distance
when he was taken prisoner, quickly and quietly, as John
Stark had been the day before. The Abenakis now had two
prisoners.

Moving along the riverbank with their captives, the
Abenakis soon saw the other two hunters coming toward
them in their canoe. Stark's captors told him to call out to
the men in the canoe and tell them to come over to his side
of the river. But Stark was determined to be a difficult captive. The Abenakis spoke their own language and French,
but did not understand English very well. When Stark
called out to his brother and Stinson, he informed them that
he and Eastman had been taken prisoner, and he told them
to paddle hard for the other shore and get away as fast as
they could. The Abenakis didn't realize that anything was
wrong until they saw the hunters in the canoe heading for
the other side of the river.

The Indians opened fire, but Stark sprang forward and
struck at their muskets, trying to throw off their aim. Most
of the shots missed, but one ball punched through William
Stark's paddle. Another ball killed David Stinson. When the

canoe reached the other side of the river, William Stark jumped out and disappeared into the woods.

Angry Abenakis crowded around John Stark, punching and kicking him. He had cost them two valuable captives.

Still, the Indians had much to show for the long journey from Canada: two captives and all the furs they had found in the hunters' camp. It was time now to return home. Stark's captors had come from a village called Odanak, on the St. Francis River between Montreal and Quebec. The Abenakis and their captives arrived at Odanak on June 9.

DEFIANT CAPTIVE

It was the custom of the Abenakis to welcome captives with a ceremony that the English called "running the gauntlet." In Odanak, the young men of the village, armed with sticks and clubs, stood facing each other in two lines. The captives were taught a little song, given a long pole to which was tied the skin of a bird or other animal, and made to run between the two lines. The Abenakis would hit them hard with their weapons. Some captives were seriously injured in these ceremonies. Stark began his run, singing his Abenaki song. After he had been struck a few times, though, he started swinging his

—**FAST FACT**—

Stark gained great respect for the Abenakis during his 1752 captivity among the Indian tribe. He later stated that he had been treated more kindly by the Abenakis than he ever knew prisoners of war to be treated by so-called civilized nations.

This illustration depicts women performing various chores in an Abenaki village. In Abenaki society, farming was considered women's work, and when ordered to help tend his captors' cornfields, a defiant John Stark refused.

pole at his tormentors. By the time he got to the end of the lines, the young Abenaki men were backing away from him to keep from being hit. Stark received only a few minor injuries. The older men in the village laughed, but some of the young men didn't find the situation so humorous.

Throughout his captivity, Stark maintained his dignity. He was given a hoe and sent to work in a cornfield. Since this was considered women's work in Abenaki culture, Stark not only hoed the weeds, but cut up the corn as well. When this didn't lead to a change in jobs, he threw his hoe into the river, stating defiantly, "It is the business of [women], and not warriors, to hoe corn." The

Abenakis admired Stark's boldness and named him "Young Chief."

In July 1752, officials from the Province of Massachusetts "redeemed," or bought the freedom of, John Stark from the Abenakis. By August, he was home again in Derryfield, New Hampshire. During his nearly two months of captivity, Stark had learned a great deal about Abenaki culture and language. He had also gained important knowledge about Indian military tactics, which he would find especially useful in the war that was coming.

2

FARM AND FOREST

To Archibald Stark and the other settlers of London-derry, New Hampshire, everything must have seemed wonderful and new. The vast forests that covered much of the Province of New Hampshire were still largely untouched by the axe and crosscut saw. Unfamiliar with the sight of men carrying muskets, herds of deer grazed serenely, and bears pawed at rotten logs in search of grubs. Beavers busied themselves damming streams and building lodges in ponds, without fear of stepping into a steel trap.

In this unspoiled world, Archibald Stark and his wife, Eleanor, believed they could start over and make a new life for themselves. The Starks had left Ireland in 1720. The voyage across the Atlantic Ocean had been long and difficult.

This stone wall still stands on the wooded property where Archibald and Eleanor Stark had their first farm in New Hampshire. John Stark was born on this property in 1728 and spent the first eight years of his life there.

Smallpox had broken out on their ship and claimed the lives of their children. When their ship arrived at Boston and word got out that there was sickness on board, neither the crew nor the passengers were allowed to come ashore. They ended up spending their first winter in America on a lonely piece of coastline in what is now the state of Maine. By the time the Starks arrived in Londonderry, New Hampshire, it would indeed be time to start over.

Archibald Stark was born in 1697 in Glasgow, Scotland, where he went to school and began to learn the carpenter's and joiner's trades. (Men who specialized in cabinetry and other fine woodwork were called joiners.) While Archibald was still a boy, his family moved to Londonderry, Ireland. There, years later, he met and married Eleanor Nichols. As Archibald and Eleanor thought about what kind of life they wanted and began to have children, they heard from friends who had moved to North America. Their friends invited them to settle in a place called New Hampshire in a region known as New England.

LIFE ON A NEW HAMPSHIRE FARM

New Hampshire was, as promised, a place of great opportunity, but the Starks knew that life there wouldn't be easy. To survive and succeed, settlers had to be smart, lucky, and willing to work. Starting a farm and keeping it going was hard work. People who lived on 18th-century farms had little time to rest and relax. The list of things that needed to be done was long and never seemed to get shorter. A house and a barn had to be built. Eventually sheds for storage would be needed, as well as a smokehouse for preserving bacon and ham. (Smokehouses were small stone or brick structures that could be tightly closed. The meat was hung inside and "cured" with the smoke of smoldering corncobs or hickory wood chips.)

Clear ground was needed to plant crops—wheat, rye, oats, and corn mostly. This meant that trees had to be cut down and the stumps pulled. The fields had to be enclosed with strong rail fences to keep out the cattle and pigs that the settlers let loose to *forage* in the woods. Then the ground was plowed. Planting followed. When, for example, wheat was

The Stark family lived in this house in Derryfield (now Manchester), New Hampshire, from 1736 to 1765.

planted, the farmer walked up and down the field, casting the grain broadly with his hand as he went. The grain was then worked into the soil with a harrow, a wooden frame with downward-pointing teeth on which the farmer stood as it was pulled by a pair of oxen. When the same crop had been planted on the same piece of ground year after year, the soil would no longer yield a good harvest, and the field had to be allowed to "rest." This meant that farmers had to clear new ground continually. In addition, the cattle, horses, pigs, and sheep needed tending, as did the vegetable garden.

There was far more work to be done than a farmer and his wife could accomplish by themselves. All young farm couples hoped to have many sons and daughters to help with the work, and the Starks were no different. They eventually had four sons: William, John, Samuel, and Archibald (and daughters whose names we do not know). The second son, John, was born at Londonderry, New Hampshire, on August 28, 1728.

CHILDHOOD AND YOUTH

John Stark was an active and intelligent young boy who enjoyed learning, but there was no school in Londonderry. Some parents didn't think that "book learning" was important. But the Starks wanted their children to be well educated, so they taught them to read and write themselves.

In 1736, the Starks' home burned and the family moved north to a piece of land on the Merrimack River at

Derryfield (today's Manchester, New Hampshire). Here John's education continued. He learned to keep accounts (records of money earned and spent) and studied history, but his parents still needed him to help on the farm.

John Stark also learned about lumber, sawmills, and the sawyer's trade. As early communities grew, there was a constant need for lumber to build houses, barns, shops, and churches. Boards were needed for walls, and thicker boards, called planks, were laid down to make floors. Wherever there was a good waterfall, a sawmill could be built. But where the power of moving water could not be harnessed, lumber had to be sawed by hand, one board at a time. To do this, a "saw log" was dragged onto a wooden platform built over a pit or on the side of a hill. Two men—one standing over the log and another under it—pulled a "pit saw" up and down until a board was cut. The work was backbreaking.

A much less laborious activity that John Stark engaged in was fishing. The Merrimack River, especially where it flowed over Amoskeag Falls, was full of fish. John and his brothers used nets and spears to catch shad weighing 20 pounds or more, sturgeon that were six feet long, alewives, salmon, and eels. Young men also enjoyed hunting and trapping, which not only put meat on the table but also brought in a little money. Some furs were always in demand. Hatters, for example, used beaver fur to make men's hats.

Hunting trips to New Hampshire's northern forests, mountains, and rivers taught young men to be tough and self-reliant. Camping in the wilderness also made them resourceful. They learned to build shelter using sticks, evergreen branches, or whatever materials were at hand. They could get a campfire going in a minute with flint and steel. If their shoes wore out, they made Indian-style moccasins from the skin of deer or moose. What they couldn't make, they did without. By the time John Stark was in his 20s, he had become an experienced hunter, trapper, and guide. Few people knew the woods as well as Stark did.

SETTLERS AND INDIANS

The settlers who lived in southern New Hampshire saw the wilderness to the north as an empty place, a kind of tree-covered desert. Yet Indians had lived, hunted, and fished there for more than a thousand years. Roads, fences, farms, and cities marked the land wherever Europeans settled, but Indians left no such traces. Because their views of the world were so different, it was hard for settlers and Indians to get along. From the time that Europeans and Indians had first come in contact with each other, there had been trouble. Sometimes the Indians had attacked families who lived on the frontier. At other times, the *provincial* government had sent soldiers to attack the Indians.

A 19th-century woodcut shows Indians attacking a colonial settlement in New Hampshire. As Europeans moved into the territories of Native American tribes, conflicts erupted.

Men such as John Stark, who spent a lot of time in the forest, knew about the Indians and their way of life. Woodsmen learned how Indians stayed alive in the wilderness and how they fought. They learned the different customs of neighboring nations of Indians, their languages, beliefs, and characteristic dress.

Many white people in 18th-century America hated and feared Indians, considering them inferior "savages." This doesn't seem to have been the case with John Stark, however. Tellingly, Stark's lasting memories of his time as a captive of the Abenakis were full of humorous incidents. Though defiant, he had apparently respected his captors—and had even enjoyed being tested by a worthy enemy who also found him worthy of respect.

3

RANGER CAPTAIN

For hundreds of years, France and Britain had been enemies. The two European countries had fought war after war. Even when they weren't fighting openly, the French and British were continually trying to undercut each other.

By the mid-18th century, France and Britain, along with Spain and the Netherlands, had achieved the status of world powers. They maintained colonies on other continents, had strong navies as well as armies, and were actively involved in trade. In North America, France controlled Canada and a large section of what is today the midwestern United States. Britain possessed 13 colonies along the continent's eastern coast.

In the first half of the 18th century, the French and British fought several wars in Europe. The fighting usually spilled over into North America, but it didn't last long there and consisted mostly of frontier raids. The farmers who settled on the New York, New Hampshire, and Massachusetts frontiers—the areas nearest to Canada—lived in fear of attacks by the French, Canadians, and Indians. French raiding parties had used the fort at Crown Point, on Lake Champlain, as a base of operations since the 1730s. Known as Fort St. Frederic to the French, it was the closest of all their forts to New York and New England and was viewed by British provincials as a real threat to safety.

By 1755, Europe was on the brink of a major war. In America, small-scale fighting between the French and British had already broken out in the contested Ohio River valley near present-day Pittsburgh. Now transport ships under full sail were speeding *regiments* of French *regulars* to Canada to fight a far bigger war, and more French troops would follow in 1756. The British, too, were busy. Soon they would assemble the largest military force ever fielded in North America. The broader European conflict, which involved a half dozen other countries in addition to France and Britain, would be called the Seven Years' War. It lasted from 1756 to 1763. In North America the fighting began in 1754 and was over by 1760. American historians usually call it the French and Indian War. To the American colonists

Fort William and Mary—located at New Castle, New Hampshire—was one of many forts built by the British to defend their colonies against French attacks. It guarded the entrance to Portsmouth Harbor.

who fought in the war, it was simply the French War or, later, the Old French War.

LIEUTENANT STARK OF ROGERS' RANGERS

Britain's northern provinces decided to combine their forces to drive the French from Crown Point. New York, Connecticut, Massachusetts, Rhode Island, and New Hampshire all formed regiments to take part in the attack. New Hampshire formed a regiment under Colonel Ephraim Blanchard. It included a ranger *company* commanded by Captain Robert Rogers. Rogers and Stark had met many times while fishing at Amoskeag Falls. Rogers was familiar

with Stark's reputation as an experienced woodsman and believed that he would make a good ranger officer. Stark was appointed a second lieutenant in Rogers' Rangers.

In the summer of 1755, Blanchard's regiment joined the army of Major General William Johnson, which was camped at Fort Lydius, an old trading post on the Hudson River north of Albany, New York. By the time Rogers' Rangers arrived at Fort Lydius, construction had begun on a new fort, which would be called Fort Edward. A road was also being cut to Lake George. The road was wide enough for ox teams to pull cannons, covered wagons loaded with supplies, and wagons that were specially designed to carry boats.

By September, Johnson's army had advanced to the southern end of Lake George. The French at Crown Point had collected a force of regulars, Canadians, and Indians, and this force was now moving south to attack Johnson's

Robert Rogers.
Commandeur der Americaner.

Stark's neighbor Robert Rogers command-ed a famous fighting force during the French and Indian War. Rogers' Rangers won a reputation for resourcefulness, toughness, and stealth. Stark, who served under Rogers, eventually commanded his own company of rangers, gaining valuable military experience. No paintings of Rogers were made while he was alive; this draw-ing was taken from a French book, circa 1778.

army. Units of the two armies collided on September 8, 1755, at the Battle of Lake George. After hours of desperate fighting, the defeated French were compelled to retreat to Crown Point.

Johnson dispatched Rogers' Rangers on a scouting mis-sion to the north to find out about French activities. When Rogers returned, he reported that the French were building a fort at Ticonderoga (which the French knew as *Carillon*). Johnson gave up on his plan to attack Crown Point. Instead he began to build a fort at the south end of Lake George, which would be named Fort William Henry. Johnson's army was disbanded in November and Stark returned home. The young lieutenant had survived his first military **campaign**.

A DIFFERENT WAY OF FIGHTING

Early in 1756, Rogers raised a new company of rangers, and John Stark was again appointed second lieutenant. By April, the company had arrived at Fort Edward and was ready for service. In the campaign of 1756, neither the French nor the British carried out any major operations on Lake George or Lake Champlain. Both armies concentrated on fort construction—the British at Fort Edward and Fort William Henry, and the French at Ticonderoga. But the rangers had other work to do.

Rangers fought a different kind of war from regulars. French and British regulars blazed away at each other with

A modern view of Fort Ticonderoga (called *Carillon* by the French) from the mouth of La Chute River to the south of the fort. Stark spent most of 1756 and 1757 scouting and skirmishing with French forces in the area around the fort.

muskets and cannons and charged with bayonets. During sieges, they dug entrenchments and stormed forts in daring night attacks. This was high-visibility warfare. The long lines of troops advancing and retreating, the colorful uniforms, the brilliantly decorated flags fluttering in the wind, and the noise and smoke of battle left an unforgettable impression.

Rangers, on the other hand, made an unimpressive appearance. They wore dark-colored or drab clothing, some of which they brought from home and some of which was provided by their captain. Jackets were short and close fitting. Hats were usually narrow brimmed and made of black felt. There was a good reason for the rangers' dull attire: their most important duty, scouting, involved not being seen. On scouting missions, rangers approached an enemy fort or camp, noted the condition of the fort or progress of construction work, counted or estimated the number of enemy troops, and perhaps took a prisoner who could be questioned. Then they returned to their own army. When a scouting mission was completely successful, the enemy would never know the rangers had been there. Skirmishes usually took place because something went wrong.

AMBUSHED NEAR TICONDEROGA

In January 1757, John Stark was part of a ranger force sent from Fort William Henry to cut off supplies that were moving by sled between the French forts at Ticonderoga and Crown Point. The rangers got into position undetected, stopped several sleds, and destroyed the supplies. However, one sled got away, and the driver made his way back to Ticonderoga. Knowing the French would come after them, the rangers headed back toward Lake George. Near Ticonderoga they were ambushed by a force of French and Indians that outnumbered them two to one. The rangers were in trouble.

When Captain Rogers was wounded twice, and Captain Spikeman was killed, John Stark found himself in command. The rangers were atop a hill, with the enemy deployed in a crescent in front of them. Rogers and others thought they should retreat right away before being completely surrounded, but Stark disagreed. Speaking firmly to the men, he told them that their hilltop position was strong and that they would defend it until nightfall,

—FAST FACT—

During the French attack on Fort William Henry in March 1757, Stark received a minor wound from a spent ball (a ball that had gone past its effective range and lost most of its force). This was the only injury he ever suffered in battle.

after which they would make their escape under cover of darkness. This was the only way they would get out of there alive, Stark said, and he would shoot the first man who tried to run away. At that moment, a French musket ball struck Stark's musket and broke it. Seeing a French soldier fall nearby, he dashed out, grabbed the soldier's musket, and returned to his position. As Stark had promised, the rangers slipped away after darkness had fallen.

After marching all night, they reached Lake George the next morning. The wounded men, suffering badly from cold and loss of blood, were too tired to march any farther. Stark realized that unless sleds could be obtained from Fort William Henry, many of his men would not survive. He immediately set out with two volunteers. They slogged through deep snow to the fort—a distance of some 32 miles—and returned the following morning with sleds to carry the men to safety.

SERVING UNDER LORD HOWE

Stark was later promoted to the rank of captain. He and his men participated in the successful defense of Fort William Henry when it was attacked by the French in March 1757. In August, however, the French captured and destroyed the fort. Having caught smallpox, Stark spent most of the campaign in bed. After recovering from the disease, he rejoined the army at Albany in October and spent the winter at Fort Edward.

In the spring of 1758, determined to drive the French from North America once and for all, the British assembled the largest army ever seen on the continent. It was at this time that Stark met Lord George Augustus Viscount

Howe. Unlike other British officers, Lord Howe saw that war in North America would be different from war in Europe. If the British expected to win this war, they would have to adapt their tactics to those of the enemy. They would have to modify their weapons, clothing, and equipment to the rough, mountainous, and heavily wooded terrain on which battles in this war were fought. Howe ordered the officers and men of his own regiment, the 55th Foot, to make many changes, and he set the example by changing his own appearance first. The soldiers of the 55th Foot cut their hair short, trimmed their three-cornered hats into narrow-brimmed "round hats," shortened their knee-length coats, and "browned" their musket barrels so that they would not reflect sunlight (and give away their position). Also, the amount of equipment each man carried was reduced. In other words, Howe tried to make his British soldiers more like rangers.

Stark didn't have a high opinion of British officers in general, but he considered Howe the best officer under whom he ever served. Most British officers looked down

—FAST FACT—

During the French and Indian War, John Stark served under the British general Lord George Augustus Viscount Howe, whom he greatly admired. Twenty years later, during the American Revolution, Stark would find himself fighting against Howe's brothers William and Richard. Sir William Howe was the commander in chief of British forces in America from 1775 to 1778. Lord Richard Howe led the British naval forces between 1776 and 1778.

their noses at provincials and made fun of them, but Howe realized that he could learn a great deal from men such as Stark. Howe set high standards for his soldiers, but he never asked anything of them that he was not willing to do himself. In action, he was a bold and aggressive commander, preferring to be out in front of his men, leading them forward. When Howe was killed in battle near Ticonderoga on July 6, 1758, Stark was devastated by the loss of his friend and mentor.

FAMILY MATTERS

Following the death of his father that same July, Stark returned home on furlough (a leave of absence). On August 20, 1758, he married Elizabeth Page.

In 1758 John Stark married Elizabeth "Molly" Page (1737–1814). Together, they had 11 children. During the American Revolution, Molly Stark served as a nurse when smallpox broke out among her husband's troops.

Stark raised a new company of rangers in 1759 and returned with the army to the Lake Champlain region. After four unsuccessful campaigns, the British finally drove the French from Ticonderoga and Crown Point that year. With the surrender of the French at Montreal in 1760, the French and Indian War effectively ended.

In the following years, John and Elizabeth Stark built a family. For Stark, this was a busy period. There was always work to be done to maintain and improve his farm and mills. Around this time, Stark also joined with others and began to develop a new settlement at Starkstown (now Dunbarton, New Hampshire).

Stark was already a well-known and highly respected community figure. He had distinguished himself in a hard-fought and bloody war. During a time of crisis, it was almost certain that others would look to him again for leadership.

4

CONTINENTAL COLONEL

At the conclusion of the Seven Years' War in 1763, the government of Great Britain faced large debts. Considerable sums had been spent protecting the 13 American colonies from the French and Indians. From the point of view of the British, it was not unreasonable to expect the provincials to pay a share of these costs. The British legislature, or Parliament, passed a series of laws imposing taxes on the American colonies. These included the Sugar Act (1763), the Stamp Act (1765), and the Townshend Acts (1767).

In the colonies, such measures created a great deal of resentment. Some colonial leaders argued that, although they were subjects of the British Crown, Parliament had no

The Stamp Act of 1765 required that a tax stamp (like the ones at right) be placed on all legal documents, permits, newspapers, and pamphlets in the American colonies. Britain's Parliament intended to use the money raised by the Stamp Act to help pay the cost of defending the colonies. Eventually, American resistance to the new tax forced Parliament to repeal the act.

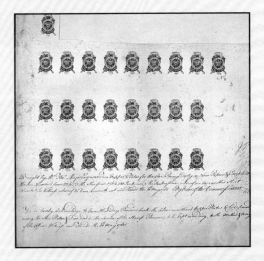

right to tax them because they weren't permitted to elect members to Parliament. Colonists frequently avoided paying the legally required taxes on imported goods, and they often harassed and intimidated the royal officials assigned to collect these customs duties. Tensions mounted, and in 1768 two British regiments arrived in Boston. The message was clear: King George III and his ministers were determined to assert the Crown's authority over the American colonies.

On April 19, 1775, the increasingly bitter political dispute between the Crown and defiant colonists took a dramatic turn. The previous evening, a large force of British regulars had marched out of Boston. Their mission: to find and destroy weapons and supplies that Massachusetts *militia* groups had stashed away in preparation for a possible fight with the *redcoats*. On the morning of the 19th, a short skirmish in the village of Lexington left a handful of

Americans dead. At a bridge outside nearby Concord, American "rebels" rained musket fire on a group of British soldiers, who retreated back into the village. Around noon, the British column re-formed for the march back to Boston, which became one long running fight. By the end of the day, pillars of white and black smoke poured from burning houses, and the crumpled bodies of dead British soldiers and American farmers lay in the roads and behind stone fences. This was no longer just a political disagreement; this was war. The American Revolution had begun.

ANSWERING THE CALL

John Stark was at work in one of his mills when news of Lexington and Concord reached him. Right away he went

The start of the American Revolution forced the British colonial governor of New Hampshire, John Wentworth (at left), to flee the colony in 1775. In place of the British authority, the rebellious Patriots established a representative legislature to rule the colony.

home, changed his clothes, mounted his horse, and galloped off for the scene of action. As he made his way south toward Massachusetts, he called all the men he met to "turn out"—that is, drop what they were doing, grab their muskets, and prepare for action. The time for talk was over. It was time to fight for liberty. Stark was known throughout New Hampshire as a strong supporter of American rights. Shortly after he reached Medford, Massachusetts, where he had told everyone to meet, Stark was joined by hundreds of armed New Hampshire men ready to fight.

It was decided that the men at Medford would be formed into a regiment. An election was held to select officers, and John Stark was the men's choice for colonel. Stark would command the regiment.

Colonel Stark and the other officers began right away to teach the men—most of whom lacked military experience—the basics of being a soldier. They taught the men to stand still when in line and to march in step. The men also learned how to load and fire their muskets together in *volleys*. If they were going to face the British in battle, they would need to know these things and much more. They would also need to be better supplied. There was a serious shortage of gunpowder. The men had only 15 *cartridges* (30 or 40 would have been better). And their muskets were made for hunting, not war. Very few of them had bayonets.

On June 3, 1775, John Stark was officially appointed colonel of the First New Hampshire Regiment.

STANDOFF AT BOSTON

More than six weeks had passed since the fighting at Lexington and Concord, and the clash between the Americans and the British had become a tense standstill. The redcoats remained in Boston, which during the 18th century lay entirely on a peninsula. The American forces—referred to at this time as the Army of Observation and composed of militia groups from Massachusetts, Rhode Island, Connecticut, and New Hampshire—had blocked the only road out of the city. The Americans had set up a series of strongly built *redoubts* along that road, which ran through the narrow Boston Neck. The British were reluctant to attempt a breakout, and the Americans didn't dare try to take the city by storm. British warships controlled the waters of Boston Harbor.

North of Boston, across about a half mile of water, lay Charlestown. The small village sat at the southernmost point of another peninsula, between the Charles and Mystic Rivers. The Charlestown peninsula also had a narrow neck and a single road leading out, which the Americans controlled. (A causeway that ran along the top of a low dam was frequently flooded, and in any case it was too small to allow large groups of soldiers to pass.) On the night of June 16,

WEAPONS OF THE 18TH-CENTURY SOLDIER

During the American Revolution, most soldiers fought with muskets and bayonets. Muskets were only accurate at close range, so soldiers had to move quite close to their enemy during battle. When fighting in an open field, the soldiers would form lines and advance. The lines fired in sections called "platoons" and "battalions." This concentrated fire was meant to disrupt the enemy's lines. If an enemy unit panicked and moved out of position, the attacking infantrymen could attach their bayonets—deadly knives, usually 15 to 20 inches long—to the ends of the muskets and charge the retreating enemy.

This style of fighting required great discipline. If soldiers became confused or ran away from an enemy charge, it could cause a break in the battle line that would imperil the entire army. Infantry soldiers needed intensive training so they could maneuver effectively in battle and stand up to bayonet charges.

This private is wearing the 1778 uniform of the First New Hampshire Regiment. In 1775, when John Stark commanded the regiment, the men had no uniforms and simply wore their own clothes.

An American musket (top), along with a socket bayonet that could be fixed to the end of the barrel to make a deadly close-range weapon. (bottom) Most British soldiers were equipped with the Short Land Service Pattern musket.

An American musket cartridge (right), made from a piece of an old letter. Soldiers usually carried 17 to 24 musket rounds into battle in a leather and wood cartridge box like the one shown.

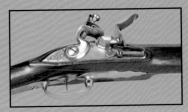

Detail of the firing mechanism of a British musket.

A bayonet (above) found on the battlefield at Guilford Courthouse.

1775, about a thousand New Englanders built a redoubt on Breed's Hill, located just to the north of Charlestown. From atop the hill, American artillery could threaten British positions in Boston. The British had to take the rebel fortification right away.

TO BREED'S HILL

On the morning of June 17, Colonel Stark received orders to send several hundred of his New Hampshire troops from Medford to Breed's Hill. The British were preparing to attack the new redoubt there. At two o'clock in the afternoon, Stark received a message that he and the rest of the New Hampshire troops were now needed. Large numbers of redcoats had begun landing on the Charlestown peninsula. When Stark and his New Hampshire men reached Charlestown Neck, they found men from other provinces wandering about aimlessly. American soldiers were blocking the road, afraid to advance. The guns of British warships boomed, raining cannon balls on Charlestown Neck. It seemed as if anyone who tried to cross the narrow strip of land would be killed. Without hesitation, Stark led his New Hampshire men forward at a steady pace. Some of them wanted to run forward to get through the naval gunfire as quickly as possible. One of Stark's officers, Captain Henry Dearborn, suggested that it might be a good idea for them to hurry on, but Stark turned to Dearborn and said, "One fresh man in action is worth ten tired ones." They would continue onward at a measured pace.

When Stark reached the redoubt on Breed's Hill, he immediately sized up the situation. The redoubt was full of men. To the left, a farm lane between two rail fences extended down the hill to the banks of the Mystic River. Connecticut troops lined most of the fence, but beyond their left, the fence was undefended. The British could push past the Americans' left *flank* and cut off their only line of retreat. Stark moved his men down the hill to fill this gap. Once there, however, he saw that the riverbank dropped off eight or nine feet to a narrow beach along the river. The enemy could get through on the beach and pass behind the American positions. Stark's men dismantled one of the rail fences and stuck the rails through the other fence, with one end pointing toward the British. As the Connecticut men to their right had done, the

Henry Dearborn served as a Continental officer in the New Hampshire Line. He began his service as a captain and fought under John Stark at Breed's Hill. Dearborn eventually rose to the rank of lieutenant colonel and fought in many major battles. He later had a distinguished career in the federal government as secretary of war.

Behind their earthworks atop Breed's Hill, Patriots commanded by Colonel William Prescott wait for the British assault, June 17, 1775. After large numbers of British troops began assembling on Charlestown peninsula to attack Prescott's position, Stark's New Hampshire regiment was summoned to reinforce the Patriots.

New Hampshire forces covered the rail fence with hay that had been stacked nearby. Such a barrier would not even slow down a musket ball, but to the British it might *look* solid. Stark directed some of his men to bring rocks down onto the beach to fill the last gap in the line. He formed his men three deep behind this crude wall and stationed himself there.

Stark gave a short speech, encouraging the men to do their duty. Within minutes the British were advancing toward them.

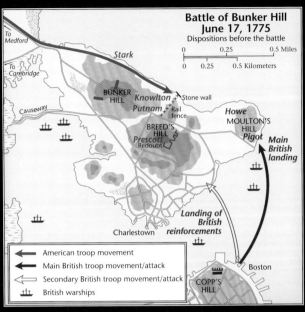

Battle of Bunker Hill
June 17, 1775
Dispositions before the battle

0   0.25   0.5 Miles

0   0.25   0.5 Kilometers

To Medford

To Cambridge

Stark

BUNKER HILL

Knowlton

Putnam

Stone wall

Rail fence

Causeway

Howe

MOULTON'S HILL

Pigot

Main British landing

BREED'S HILL

Prescott

Redoubt

Landing of British reinforcements

Charlestown

→ American troop movement

→ Main British troop movement/attack

⇐ Secondary British troop movement/attack

⚓ British warships

Boston

COPP'S HILL

First Attack

BUNKER HILL

MOULTON'S HILL

Causeway

BREED'S HILL

Charlestown

0   0.25   0.5 Miles

0   0.25   0.5 Kilometers

CORP'S HILL

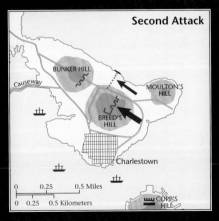

Second Attack

BUNKER HILL

Causeway

MOULTON'S HILL

BREED'S HILL

Charlestown

0   0.25   0.5 Miles

0   0.25   0.5 Kilometers

CORP'S HILL

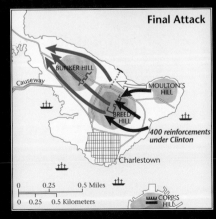

Final Attack

BUNKER HILL

Causeway

MOULTON'S HILL

BREED'S HILL

400 reinforcements under Clinton

Charlestown

0   0.25   0.5 Miles

0   0.25   0.5 Kilometers

CORP'S HILL

The British plan called for a coordinated attack across the length of the American positions, but the assault would be concentrated along the American left, at the rail fence and on the beach. The British units that broke through there would wheel toward Breed's Hill, attacking the American redoubt from the flank as other units pressed in from the front.

"THICK AS SHEEP IN A FOLD"

Unfortunately for the British, the American left didn't give way. The redcoat columns moving against Stark's New Hampshire men on the beach encountered especially deadly resistance. When the redcoats got within 40 or 50 yards, Stark's men opened fire. Every man fired and reloaded as fast as he could. When the British fell back and the smoke cleared, scores of redcoats lay wounded or dead in front of the stone wall. Along the rail fence and all the way up Breed's Hill, the British had been forced to pull back with heavy losses.

The redcoats mounted a second attack but were once again repulsed. On the beach in front of Stark's men, a British officer remarked, the dead "lay as thick as sheep in a fold."

A third attack was ordered, but this time British commanders decided against trying to break through the American left. The bulk of the British force was flung at the redoubt on Breed's Hill. Watching from the beach along the Mystic River, John Stark saw that the redcoats were about to overrun the redoubt. He realized that it was time to pull his men back. As they withdrew, Stark's men provided covering fire for the Americans retreating from Breed's Hill.

By dusk the British had accomplished their objective, having taken the redoubt on Breed's Hill and forced the Americans off the peninsula as far as Charlestown Neck. But they had suffered shockingly high *casualties*. More than 1,000 British soldiers—about half the total number engaged at the misleadingly named Battle of Bunker Hill—were killed or wounded. The Americans, meanwhile, suffered an estimated 450 casualties.

OFFICER IN THE CONTINENTAL ARMY

In early July, George Washington arrived in Cambridge, Massachusetts, to take command of the American forces. The Second Continental Congress, meeting in Philadelphia, had appointed Washington commander in chief of a unified army of regular soldiers, which would come to be called the Continental Army.

But the siege of Boston continued throughout the summer and fall of 1775. At the end of the year, enlistments expired and the First New Hampshire Regiment was disbanded. On January 1, 1776, John Stark was appointed colonel of the Fifth Continental Regiment. His new regiment was sent to New York City in the spring. Then it was ordered north to Crown Point and Ticonderoga. The New Hampshire troops were building huts on Mount Independence, across Lake Champlain from Ticonderoga, when news was received in July that Congress had declared the 13 colonies to be the United States, free and independent of Britain. When a copy of the Declaration of Independence was read to the troops at Ticonderoga, the men cheered.

Stark and his men marched south in November to join General Washington in Pennsylvania. He took part in the Battle of Trenton on December 26, 1776.

With the end of the year, enlistments again expired. After returning to New Hampshire in early 1777 to raise a new regiment, Stark received news that Congress had promoted several colonels to the rank of brigadier general in the Continental Army. Although he was New Hampshire's senior colonel, Stark had been passed over for promotion while another, less experienced New Hampshire officer, Enoch Poor, was now commander of a Continental *brigade*. Stark was shocked. He was not one to hold a grudge, but he knew that there were men in Congress who didn't like him. He decided to resign. Other Continental officers, his closest friends, couldn't talk him out of it. Stark was as deeply committed to the cause as ever, but his sense of honor made it impossible for him to remain in the service. He told his friends that "an officer who would not maintain his rank, was unworthy to serve his country."

5

BENNINGTON

In June 1777, a large British army commanded by General John Burgoyne moved south out of Canada. Burgoyne's plan was to capture Ticonderoga, defeat the Continental forces in the area, and march on to Albany. There, he would be joined by another British army, which was to move up the Hudson River from New York City. This would create a line of British posts extending from New York City to Montreal, Canada. The New England states would be cut off from New York and the states to the south. If this plan worked, the British would probably win the war.

In the spring of 1777, Continental Army recruiters were having trouble finding men. Few were willing to sign up,

As the British general John Burgoyne marched south from Canada during the summer of 1777, his army of about 8,000 British soldiers, German mercenaries, and Indian warriors won a series of victories. Burgoyne's goal was Albany, the capital of New York, which he had promised King George III he would capture and occupy by the fall.

especially now that **Continentals** had to serve for three years or for the whole war. Ticonderoga was a large post. Defending it properly would take at least 10,000 men, but in June there were fewer than 3,000. When Burgoyne's army began to surround Ticonderoga, the Continental officers agreed that it would be better to save the army than to save the post. On the night of July 5, the Americans abandoned Ticonderoga. Burgoyne pursued, and on July 7, about 1,000 of his troops clashed with American units covering the Continental retreat. After a bitter battle during which both sides suffered heavy casualties, the American rear guard was defeated.

As news of Ticonderoga's fall spread, many **Patriots** were shocked. It had been widely assumed that the fort was too strong to be taken. In New England, shock soon turned into panic. Along the frontier, Indians who had joined Burgoyne's army were fanning out over the countryside, killing, looting, and burning. The Continental Army in the North, known as the Northern Department, seemed incapable of stopping Burgoyne's advance.

RAISING A BRIGADE

Meeting in Exeter in July, members of New Hampshire's legislature feared that nothing stood between the enemy and the people of their state. The legislators recognized that they needed to raise regiments of *levies* to protect New Hampshire. But New Hampshire was a poor state. It had already spent a great deal of money raising, equipping, feeding, and paying troops, and there was no money left.

John Langdon, a wealthy businessman from Portsmouth, loaned the government of New Hampshire money to equip John Stark's militia so that it could successfully engage Burgoyne. Langdon also served with the militia as an officer under Stark, as well as in other campaigns during the Revolution. After the war, he was a delegate to the Constitutional Convention, was elected to the U.S. Senate, and served as governor of New Hampshire.

John Langdon, a wealthy merchant, delegate to the Second Continental Congress, and speaker of the New Hampshire House, offered a solution. Langdon informed his fellow legislators that he had $3,000, which he would be willing to loan the state. Furthermore, he would pledge his silver dishes and eating utensils for the same amount. He also promised to sell 70 large casks of rum for as much money as he could get. If New Hampshire took him up on the offer and the British were stopped, Langdon said, the state could pay him back. If the plan failed, he would have no need of such things as money or property anyway. "We can raise a brigade," he declared, "and our friend Stark, who so nobly sustained the honor of our arms at Bunker's Hill, may safely be entrusted with the command, and we will check Burgoyne."

Stark agreed to command the brigade as long as no one tried to tell him how to do his job. He would consider himself responsible only to the state of New Hampshire. When people heard that Stark would lead the troops that were being raised, recruits rushed to sign up.

BAUM'S MISSION

As General Burgoyne's army worked its way south toward Saratoga during the summer of 1777, it began to have supply problems. In August, Burgoyne decided to dispatch an expedition to find food, horses, and other items his army desperately needed. At Bennington, Vermont, there were

This color drawing shows the uniforms worn by soldiers in the Brunswick Regiment of Dragoons, which formed the main body of Lieutenant Colonel Friedrich Baum's detachment. Baum's orders were to invade Vermont and find food and supplies desperately needed by Burgoyne's army.

storehouses full of beef and flour, and the small town was thought to be protected by only a few hundred New England militiamen. Philip Skene, a prominent New York *Loyalist* and Burgoyne's political adviser, assured the general that not only would the militiamen retreat at the sight of his troops, but Loyalists in the area would come forward to join the advancing British army.

Burgoyne assigned the foraging mission to Lieutenant Colonel Friedrich Baum. Baum's detachment of more than 700 men included Loyalists, Indians, Canadians, and British regulars. But the backbone of the force consisted of German professional soldiers (or "Hessians," as the Americans called them). Most were dragoons, heavily armed mounted troops, who in this case had to march on foot because of the shortage of horses in Burgoyne's army. Sharpshooters known as Jägers rounded out Baum's Hessians. On August 11, Baum and his contingent split off from Burgoyne's main army near Fort Edward and began moving southeast toward Bennington.

STARK MOVES INTO POSITION

Two days earlier, John Stark had arrived in the town of Manchester, north of Bennington, where he was assembling his New Hampshire brigade. There Stark encountered Major General Benjamin Lincoln of the Continental Army. General Lincoln had orders to gather all available militiamen to supplement the small Continental force in the area. He informed Stark of this fact, but Stark replied that he didn't take orders from Continental Army officers. He was responsible only to the state of New Hampshire and would wage his own campaign against General Burgoyne. Fortunately for the American cause, Lincoln didn't press the matter.

Stark proceeded to march his troops to Bennington. On August 13, he received word that a party of Indians was about 12 miles away, at Cambridge, New York, and was heading toward Bennington. Stark sent out a detachment of 200 men, under Lieutenant Colonel Gregg, to meet the Indians. Later in the day, Stark received news that a large enemy force was moving his way.

On August 14, Stark marched his brigade and some militia to the west of Bennington to engage the enemy. About four miles outside the town, they encountered Gregg's detachment in full retreat. The 200-man scouting party had run into Baum's larger force, which was now

Benjamin Lincoln, a general in the Continental Army, tried to bring Stark's levies under his control. Had Stark agreed, his men probably would not have been in position to stop Baum's foraging mission.

in hot pursuit of the Americans. With the arrival of Stark's brigade, Baum stopped his pursuit and deployed his men on high ground overlooking the Walloomsac River. Anchoring Baum's position was a high hill that the German dragoons and British riflemen began fortifying.

Stark brought his troops into line on a hill opposite the dragoons. When Baum declined to attack, Stark moved his force back about a mile and encamped. The men did not have tents, so they made "bush huts" to sleep in, using bushes and tree branches.

DECISIVE ENGAGEMENT

Heavy rains prevented a battle on the 15th, though Stark did send out skirmishers to harass the enemy. The following morning, Stark's force was swelled by the arrival of militia from Vermont and Massachusetts. The rains continued until about noon, after which the clouds broke and the sun came out.

Around three o'clock in the afternoon, the American attack began. Stark had planned a four-pronged assault, with troops attacking the enemy from the front, right and left flanks, and rear. The Americans' spirits were high. The men pushed forward, cheering and pouring volley after volley into the enemy lines. Most of Baum's troops broke and ran for their lives, with frenzied American militiamen pursuing them through the woods in every direction. But the dra-

New Hampshire soldiers overrun an enemy position during the Battle of Bennington. Before the battle, Stark reportedly shouted to his men, "Boys, yonder are the Red Coats. Before night they are ours or Molly Stark sleeps a widow."

goons on the hill put up a desperate fight. When they ran out of ammunition, the Hessians went at the Americans with their swords. After Baum was mortally wounded, however, the surrounded and outnumbered dragoons surrendered.

The American victory seemed complete. But then Stark received an alarming report: a large enemy column was just two miles away and moving quickly toward the battlefield. Burgoyne had sent the column—an 800-man force composed mostly of Hessians and commanded by Lieutenant Colonel Heinrich von Breymann—to reinforce Baum. Though it was too late to fulfill that mission, Breymann

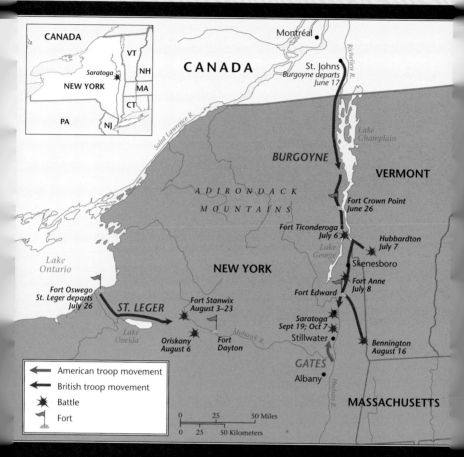

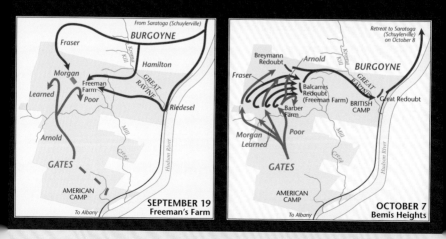

General John Burgoyne's 1777 invasion from Canada (above) was crippled by Stark's victory at Bennington. After major engagements at Freeman's Farm and Bemis Heights (below), Burgoyne surrendered at Saratoga on October 17.

might still deal a terrible blow to the Americans. With a large part of his force scattered throughout the woods in pursuit of survivors of Baum's detachment, Stark would be hard pressed to meet the new threat.

Just when it seemed that Stark's victory might turn into defeat, a regiment of Continentals under the command of Seth Warner arrived. His troops thus reinforced, Stark was able to fend off the Hessian attack. At the sound of renewed gunfire, Stark's scattered militiamen rushed to rejoin the main group of Americans. In the fighting that followed, Breymann's force came close to suffering the same fate as Baum's.

—FAST FACT—

Before leading his men in the attack on the dragoons' redoubt at the Battle of Bennington, Stark tied his horse to a post by a wooden bridge over the Walloomsac River. During the battle, someone stole the brown mare.

After darkness fell, however, the Hessian commander managed to organize a retreat that saved his detachment from annihilation.

Still, the Battle of Bennington had been a brilliant American victory. Baum's detachment had been wiped out, with only a handful of exhausted men staggering back to the main British camp, and Breymann's had been sent reeling. Stark's men had captured four cannons, as well as wagons, horses, and muskets. Most important, Burgoyne's army had lost more than 900 men—over 200 killed and 700 captured—in a single day. Numerous others had been wounded in the fighting. On the American side, casualties had been light, with about 30 killed and 40 wounded.

AFTERMATH

Burgoyne was paralyzed by the defeat. Before Bennington, he had enjoyed victory after victory, but now he began to feel hemmed in by the quickly gathering American forces. Just two months later, with his army surrounded and out of supplies, Burgoyne would be compelled to surrender to the Continentals at Saratoga. That proved to be one of the turning points of the Revolution.

In the weeks following the Battle of Bennington, which made possible the decisive victory at Saratoga, Stark received many letters of congratulations. Hoping that he would be willing to forget their "disagreement," Congress made Stark a brigadier general in the Continental Army on October 4, 1777.

6

REVOLUTIONARY HERO

Brigadier General John Stark was twice given command of the troops and posts on New York's northern frontier, first in 1778 and again in 1781. The frontier extended from Fort Schuyler (present-day Rome, New York), eastward along the Mohawk River to Albany, then northward along the Hudson River to Lake George. To guard this vast territory, Stark and other officers were rarely given more than two Continental regiments.

Considering the importance of the region to the war effort, it might seem surprising that more troops were not sent. But there were no troops to send. The Continental Army continually faced a shortage of men because of expiring enlistments, sickness, desertion (leaving the army

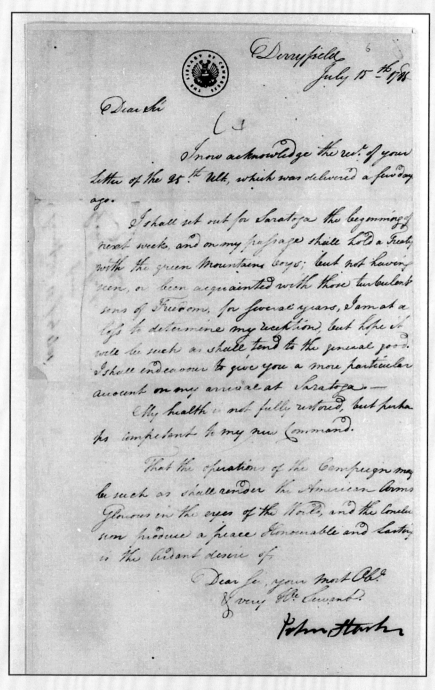

In this July 15, 1781, letter to George Washington, Stark mentions his promotion to command of the Continental Army's Northern Department, which occurred three weeks earlier. This was the second time Stark had been placed in charge of this important area.

without permission), and battle losses. Continental regiments were needed at other posts.

Most of the people who once lived on the northern frontier had fled the region. But the wheat that was grown by those who remained, especially in the Mohawk Valley, was important to the army. Mills ground the wheat into flour, which the Continental Army bought and the soldiers made into bread or dumplings. Cattle raised in the region ended up as beef boiling in camp kettles.

In Canada, Loyalists who had formerly lived along the upper New York frontier looked for every opportunity to wreak havoc in the region. Small parties of Loyalists and Indians were always roaming the region, hoping to kill Patriots and destroy the mills, farms, crops, and livestock of their enemies. Almost every year, the British organized major raids designed to ruin the rebels' ability to raise wheat and cattle. In many areas, Continentals could not venture into the forest to cut firewood without fear of being killed or captured. They were little more than prisoners in their own forts.

Stark was frustrated that he didn't have the resources to better protect the frontier. He believed in taking direct action, but sometimes his only recourse was to write letters pleading for help. In an October 1781 letter, Stark informed New York's governor, George Clinton, "My patience is already exhausted in making fruitless applications to the officers, acting by the authority of Congress, to procure supplies. They either will not, or can not, grant them. I have now no other recourse than to make application to you, who seem to be more interested in the protection of this frontier than any other man—being the father and guardian of the people." Stark warned the governor that if the frontier posts were not supplied, they would have to be evacuated as far as Albany—and perhaps even that important town would have to be given up to the enemy. Whatever the state of New York could do, Stark hoped that it would "save this unhappy frontier from ruin." Stark's letters as northern frontier commander are full of such pleas.

From 1779 to the end of 1780, Stark commanded a brigade of four regiments from Connecticut, Rhode Island, and Massachusetts. From January 1781 to the spring of 1783, he commanded the New Hampshire Brigade. Unlike militia and levies, Continental troops did not get to go home after a few weeks of service. They were in the field every day, year after year, until

New York governor George Clinton received numerous letters from Stark, asking for food for his soldiers serving in New York. With little money in the state treasury, Clinton did not have the means to purchase supplies for Stark's men.

Between 1776 and 1783, Stark some-times worked with General John Sullivan (pictured), whom he liked and respected. Like Stark, Sullivan was from New Hamp-shire; he would later serve as governor and represent the state in Congress.

their term of enlistment was up or until the war ended. Good brigade commanders, such as Stark, were constantly with their troops. They knew many of their men by name and understood what they were going through every day. They marched the same roads, ate the same food (and sometimes starved together), fought and bled together in battle, and suffered together through bitter cold, blistering heat, and every other kind of weather.

"INSULTS & NEGLECTS"

As the war progressed, the Continental soldiers became more and more isolated from the people they protected and from the governments that were supposed to feed, clothe, and pay them. Again and again, the officials responsible for making sure the men got what they needed—and what they had been promised—failed to do so. Cold and hungry sol-diers often marched off to do their duty in ragged clothes and worn-out shoes, sometimes leaving bloody footprints in the snow. In most cases soldiers had no one to turn to but their officers, yet even good officers such as Stark could do little to ease the plight of their men.

"The Insults & Neglects which the Army have met with from the Country," one of Stark's officers wrote in a bitter 1780 letter to his brother, "Beggers all description, it must Go no farther they can endure it no longer . . . I am in Rags, have lain in the Rain on the Ground for 40 hours past, & only a Junk of fresh Beef & that without Salt to dine on this day, rec'd no pay since last December . . . & all this for my Cowardly Countrymen who flinch at the very time when their Exertions are wanted, & hold their Purse Strings as tho

British spy John André was hanged in October 1780 for his part in a plot with American traitor Benedict Arnold to turn over the fort at West Point to the British. John Stark served on the military court that found André guilty and sentenced him to death.

they would Damn the World, rather than part with a Dollar to their Army."

General Stark, too, had grown angry watching his officers and men struggle along without pay. Writing to a friend in the New Hampshire state government in December 1780, he asked, "What must be the feelings of a number of Officers, who have now got leave to go & see their Familys & friends; and not a shilling of money to support their expenses? And if they do go, must assume the Characters of Beggars. . . . Perseverance has long been their favorite topic, and hope almost their only support; but those are now in a manner banished, and despair . . . stares them boldly in the face."

As the campaign of 1781 ground to a close, Stark's outlook darkened. In command of the New Hampshire Brigade at Saratoga (today's Schuylerville, New York), Stark had to report to his superior, General William Heath, that of the two regiments under his command (about 400 men), only 36 men were fit for duty. "The remainder are so naked," Stark wrote to Heath at West Point, "that they cannot procure fuel [firewood] for their own use." Congress had declared December 13, 1781, to be a day of thanksgiving for the surrender of the British at Yorktown, Virginia, in October. In a postscript to his letter to Heath, Stark wrote, "I never saw a thanksgiving before that was so melancholy. I may, I believe with safety, affirm that there will not be a thankful heart in this garrison, nor one that has cause to be satisfied with his circumstances. It may be argued that it is a blessing to have trials; but life without enjoyment, and replete with misery, is rather (in my opinion) a curse than a blessing."

"LIVE FREE OR DIE"

The Revolutionary War officially ended in September 1783, with the signing of the Treaty of Paris. Stark had left the army the previous June. During the final years of the war, he had suffered from rheumatism (a painful inflammation of the joints) and had gotten permission to spend winters at home.

Now he was home for good. There, as he later described it, he devoted his time "entirely to domestic employments." Stark had the joy of a large family, but also the sadness of outliving his wife and all but two of his children (his oldest, Caleb, born in 1759, and his youngest, Sophia, born in 1782).

—FAST FACT—

Many histories of the American Revolution imply that the war ended with the British surrender at Yorktown on October 19, 1781. But the Continental Army, including General Stark and the New Hampshire Line, remained in the field for two more years.

For many years, the people of Bennington, Vermont, commemorated the Revolutionary War battle on its anniversary, August 16. John Stark, who didn't travel much in his later years, declined many invitations to attend the event. But it became something of a tradition for the orga-

This statue of John Stark guards the entrance to the state capitol building in Concord, New Hampshire.

nizers to read a letter written by the general for the occasion. In 1809, Stark enclosed with his letter a toast, which read, "Live Free or Die; Death Is Not the Worst of Evils." The

John Stark's grave is located in a memorial park in Manchester, New Hampshire.

first part of this toast would later be adopted as the New Hampshire state motto.

Though age and illness gradually limited his abilities, Stark's memory of the French and Indian War remained clear and detailed. Yet in his final years, he remembered very little of the Revolution. When someone asked him a question about the Battle of Bunker Hill, he answered, "All I know about it is, that we gained the victory."

General John Stark died on May 8, 1822. Today, the name of this hero of the Revolutionary War has largely been forgotten. But among earlier generations of Americans, Stark's key role in securing the nation's indepen-

—FAST FACT—

At the time of his death in 1822, John Stark was the last surviving general of the American Revolution.

dence was widely recognized. "The victories of Bennington—the first link in the chain of successes which issued in the surrender at Saratoga—are still fresh in the memory of every American," President Thomas Jefferson wrote in 1805, "and the name of him who achieved them dear to his heart."

Chronology

1728: John Stark is born in Londonderry, New Hampshire, on August 28.

1736: The Stark family moves to Derryfield.

1752: On a hunting trip, Stark is captured by a party of Abenaki Indians. He is released two months later.

1754: The French and Indian War begins.

1755: Stark is appointed a lieutenant in the New Hampshire provincial forces and serves with Rogers' Rangers.

1757: Promoted to captain and given command of a ranger company; is stricken with smallpox but recovers.

1758: Stark's company joins the British army at Lake George. The British expedition to capture the French fort at Ticonderoga fails. Stark's father dies on July 25. Stark marries Elizabeth Page on August 20.

1759: Raises a new company and joins Amherst's army at Fort Edward. The French are driven from Ticonderoga and Crown Point. Stark's first son, Caleb, is born December 3.

1760: With the surrender of the French army at Montreal, the war in North America ends. Stark returns home.

1761: Son Archibald is born May 28.

1763: Son John is born April 17, but dies shortly afterward.

1765: Daughter Eleanor is born May 4.

1767: Another daughter, Eleanor "junior," is born June 30 but soon dies. The older Eleanor dies in August.

1769: Daughter Sarah is born June 11.

1771: Daughter Elizabeth is born August 10.

1773: Daughter Mary is born September 19.

1775: On April 19, the battles of Lexington and Concord signal the beginning of the American Revolution. Stark is appointed colonel of the First New Hampshire Regiment, which he commands at the Battle of Bunker Hill on June 17. Son Charles is born December 2.

1776: Appointed colonel of the Fifth Continental Regiment on

January 1. Joins the main army at New York, then is sent to reinforce the northern army at Crown Point. In November, rejoins the main army under Washington in Pennsylvania. Leads his regiment at the Battle of Trenton, December 26.

1777: When a less experienced officer is promoted ahead of him, Stark resigns from the Continental Army. In July, the government of New Hampshire makes him a brigadier general and places him in command of its levies. Stark achieves his greatest victory at the Battle of Bennington, August 16. On October 4, Congress makes Stark a Continental brigadier general.

1778: In command on the northern New York frontier.

1779: Commands a brigade of Continental troops from Massachusetts, Connecticut, and Rhode Island. Occupies Newport, Rhode Island, after the British evacuate the city. Joins the main army in New Jersey.

1780: Stark's brigade takes part in the Battle of Springfield, New Jersey. In November, Stark leads a 2,000-man detachment into enemy territory north of New York City to forage for supplies for the army. Suffering from rheumatism, he returns to Derryfield to recover his health.

1781: After a reorganization of the army, Stark is placed in command of the New Hampshire Brigade. Commands the troops on the northern New York frontier. Because of rheumatism, he again spends the winter at home.

1782: Despite ongoing health challenges, remains in command of the New Hampshire Brigade.

1783: The American Revolution officially ends, and the Continental Army is disbanded. Stark returns to his farm in Derryfield.

1786: Congress makes Stark an honorary major general.

1791: Son Archibald dies on September 11, at the age of 30.

1814: Wife, Elizabeth, dies on June 29.

1822: John Stark dies on May 8.

Glossary

brigade—a large military unit consisting of two or more regiments and commanded by a brigadier general.

campaign—a connected series of military actions that make up a phase of a war.

cartridge—a casing, formerly a paper tube about the size of a man's finger, containing a projectile and charge of gunpowder.

casualties—soldiers who are killed, wounded, captured, or missing in action during a battle.

company—a military unit, usually commanded by a captain, that during the colonial and Revolutionary War periods might contain anywhere from 60 to 100 men when at full strength.

Continentals—regular soldiers recruited in each state under the authority of the Continental Congress; the army formed of these soldiers during the American Revolution was known as the Continental Army or Continental Line.

flank—the left or right side of a military force formed for battle.

forage—to search for food.

levies—men who were enlisted from the militia during the American Revolution to serve in specially formed regiments for a limited time; regiments of levies were raised by the states to reinforce the Continental Army or defend the frontiers.

Loyalist—an American who remained loyal to the king and the British government during the Revolutionary War.

militia—civilian men between the ages of 16 and 60 who were required by law to arm and equip themselves, attend training sessions, and turn out for military service (usually lasting from a few days to a few weeks) when called upon by their officers.

Patriot—a supporter of American independence during the Revolutionary War.

province—a colony; Britain's North American colonies were usually called provinces.

provincial—relating to one of Britain's North American provinces; a resident of one of the provinces.

redcoats—British soldiers during the Revolutionary War.

redoubt—a small, usually temporary enclosed fortification that was typically made of earth and other handy materials, such as tree trunks, rails from wooden fences, and stones.

regiment—a military unit, usually commanded by a colonel, that consisted of 6 to 13 companies.

regulars—professional soldiers.

smallpox—a disease caused by a virus that produced frequent, deadly epidemics before widespread vaccination.

volley—a coordinated, simultaneous firing of weapons.

Further Reading

Books for Students:

Moore, Kay. *If You Lived at the Time of the American Revolution*. Illustrated by Daniel O'Leary. New York: Scholastic, 1998.

Murray, Stuart. *Eyewitness: American Revolution*. New York: Dorling Kindersley Publishing, 2002.

Strum, Richard. *Causes of the American Revolution*. Stockton, N.J.: OTTN Publishing, 2005.

Books for Older Readers:

Ketchum, Richard M. *Decisive Day*. New York: Henry Holt & Co., 1962.

————. *Saratoga: Turning Point of America's Revolutionary War*. New York: Henry Holt & Co., 1997.

Moore, Howard Parker. *A Life of General John Stark of New Hampshire*. (Self-published, 1949.)

Stark, Caleb. *Memoir and Official Correspondence of General John Stark, with Notices of Several Other Officers of the Revolution*. 1860. Reprint Westminster, Md.: Heritage Books, Inc., 1999.

http://www.virtualvermont.com/index.php?loc=http://
www.virtualvermont.com/history/jstark.html

A short biography of John Stark, from an Internet magazine focusing on Vermont life and history.

http://seacoastnh.com/Famous_People/Framers_of_
Freedom/John_Stark/

A brief account of the life of John Stark, who is among more than a dozen other famous New Hampshire "Framers of Freedom" profiled by this site.

http://www.britishbattles.com/battle-bennington.htm

This Web page, which provides a good overview of the Battle of Bennington, includes a map and several illustrations.

http://www.thewarthatmadeamerica.org

The companion site to the 2006 PBS series *The War That Made America,* about the French and Indian War, includes an interactive time line, biographies, interesting historical notes, and links to other resources.

Index

Numbers in **bold italics** refer to captions.

Picture Credits

About the Author

KARL LEWIS CRANNELL was born December 16, 1953, in Glens Falls, New York. His lifelong affinity with history began at birth when his parents paid the hospital bill with funds from the sale of an 18th-century bear trap which his father found in the woods. At age nine, he painted a large eye on his snow saucer to make a Greek shield. He is currently leading a group of volunteers in constructing a faithful reproduction of a Revolutionary War–period soldiers' hut at Fort Ticonderoga.

Crannell majored in music performance at the Crane School of Music, and literature at SUNY Potsdam, from which he graduated in 1978. He is employed at Fort Ticonderoga as Public Programs Coordinator, and conducts educational outreach programs as "Sgt. Crannell of the 4th Pennsylvania Regt." He lives at the edge of the Carillon battlefield with his wife, Amy, and their feral Manx cat, Nubbin.